This book is dedicated to our children, Joel, Jethro, Joseph, and Jessica. Also to other children who have been abused, molested, abandoned, and abducted, regardless of their race, colour, or ethnicity, who have been unjustly removed from their homes into care without consideration. And also to parents who love their children but were unjustly persecuted or imprisoned by the governments of their countries just for being a parent the way they know how.

TIME BOMBS ARE TICKING IN UK

Watch Out!

JOE T. A. NWOKOYE

Library of Congress Control Number: 2015905140
ISBN: Hardcover   978-1-4990-9660-6
               Softcover   978-1-4990-9661-3
               eBook   978-1-4990-9662-0

KJV
Scripture quotations marked KJV are from the Holy Bible, King James Version (Authorized Version). First published in 1611. Quoted from the KJV Classic Reference Bible, Copyright © 1983 by the Zondervan Corporation.

Any people depicted in stock imagery provided by Thinkstock are models, and such images are being used for illustrative purposes only.
Certain stock imagery © Thinkstock.

Cover designer: Ikenna O. Aghanya
                iyke70@gmail

Print information available on the last page.

Rev. date: 04/17/2015

To order additional copies of this book, contact:
Xlibris
800-056-3182
www.Xlibrispublishing.co.uk
Orders@Xlibrispublishing.co.uk
708246

CONTENTS

FOREWORD

We live in a world ruled by Satan, the 'prince of this world', as Jesus called him. It is a world that tells Bible-believing Christians that we need to mind our own business and keep our beliefs and values to ourselves. We are told, 'To each his own' and 'Live and let live.' At best, we are admonished to exercise 'tolerance' towards everyone, regardless of how contrary or contradictory their belief system and, indeed, their actions may be to our own. At worst, we Christians may be subject to active persecution simply because of what we believe and how we live our lives. The persecution that we suffer may be verbal—mockery of and disrespect for the very beliefs that we hold most dear. Or at the other extreme, persecution may be far more severe, taking such forms as imprisonment, violence against us, or even threats of death itself.

It seems to follow that the more we believers are willing to stand for our faith, the more persecution we can expect to experience. However, if you make the choice each day to stand boldly for what you believe in, to fearlessly proclaim Jesus as the one and only way to have a relationship with God, and to courageously live out your faith in a world that is becoming more and more hostile to followers of Christ, then persecution, perhaps to the very highest levels, is certain to follow.

In this book, my friend Pastor Joe Nwokoye relates a very personal story of the struggle and persecution that he and his family experienced because of his Christian faith and his fearless stand for God and for what God teaches in His Word, the Bible. By all means, as you read this book, imagine if this was to happen to you or your loved ones. But as you do, don't miss the warning that is inherent to this narrative: Satan is alive and well and, as a prowling lion, is seeking, every second, to steal, kill, and destroy the work of God and the people who are courageous enough to take a stand for Him.

Yes, the world in which we live is not a safe or friendly place for Christians. We are reminded of this in John 16:33 (NIV) by Jesus, who warned, 'In this world you *will* have trouble.' But the good news that we celebrate is found in the encouraging words that Jesus seemed to add quickly onto that statement when He said, 'But take heart! I have overcome the world.' May you read this book with open eyes, an open heart, and an open mind. As you do, I pray that God richly blesses each of you, just as He has blessed those of us who have the privilege of knowing Pastor Joe.

Dr Randall W. Harper
Lewiston, Idaho, USA

ACKNOWLEDGEMENTS

My utmost gratitude goes to God Almighty, who is keeping me alive and who gave me the grace and wisdom to write this book.

I thank God for my wonderful family, who are always very supportive. My long-time friends in the ministry whose fellowship I value very much: Dr Bill Matthews, Bishop Paul Fadeyi, Dr Peter Asiamah, Pastor Ladell Graham, Pastor Ernest Khokhar, and also my trusted partners in ministry Dr and Mrs Randy Harper, Harry and Linda, Jason and Katie, Daniel and Crystal, Kathy McCarthy, Eldon and Marilyn Riggle, Nancy Luetchens, and Denny Blewett. Special thanks to all of you who are supporting the vision and mission of Zion Praise Centre. Thanks to the church council of ZPC and all the lecturers of ZBI. I appreciate Dr and Mrs Ticon Nwokoye for their friendship. I am grateful to my cousin Comrade Gabriel Nwobu for his input. I thank you, Annabelle Manoukian, for working so hard in typing this book. Last but not least, my legal adviser, Michelle Renton, who has been my trusted lawyer for many years. May the gracious Lord bless you all.

CHAPTER 1

Wickedness and Possession

The United Kingdom has been faced with many stories of people abusing children. Some of these people were those in positions of authority. I guess this wicked practice may never be eradicated, but something must be done and done fast by the appropriate authorities to help and save the lives of vulnerable and innocent children. Recently, we had a situation where there were two mothers who were serving in Cornton Vale Prison; one stabbed her three beautiful children to death in order to hurt the children's father, while the other one killed her son and dumped him in the woods but did not kill the other kids. There is no amount of prison sentence that would bring those children back. If these mothers were living in the United States, they might have faced electric chairs, and that also would not bring these children back. What a tragedy. Something must be done fast.

We hear stories after stories like these two examples up and down the country. We hear about how our elderly folks are being repeatedly abused by the people who should be taking care of them in some care homes. How about our young boys or youth who were molested by gay priests and some celebrities?

Wickedness

Proverbs 29:16

Dictionary definition—Quality of being evil or morally wrong.

Biblical definition—In Luke 11:39 and Psalm 7:11, the Bible tells us that wickedness is the things of the inner heart. So a person can dress wonderfully well, wear the most expensive perfume, live in a mansion, and drive an expensive car, but his or her heart may be full of wickedness. This is where I would categorize those people who abuse our elderly by denying them simple care such as food, hygiene, and so on.

Perversion

Dictionary definition—Unnatural, perverse behaviour, one with a sexual perversion.

People in these categories prey on young boys and girls who trust them. Examples are gay priests and some perverse celebrities who have strong influence on these young ones who were placed under their care. I have seen a case where a father had sexually abused his own child.

Possession

Dictionary definition—Someone who is controlled by a negative spirit; under the control of evil spirits; madness.

People in these categories are like those two mothers who were serving in prison for killing their children. If a mother or a father, for whatever reason, could kill their children, they are possessed. In my opinion, anybody who could take another person's life at will, especially that of those that cannot defend themselves, is possessed by evil spirits. In the political world, some dictators are possessed by evil spirits because their actions are abnormal.

Many of these leaders, both dead and alive, were intoxicated with power. Some were military dictators while others were elected by rigged ballots. These individuals were not born as dictators; they were normal children born into normal families, and some were born into abject poverty. Almost in every case, these individuals were brainwashed by mentors or dictators whose ideas, principles, and ideologies they wanted to emulate. Most dictators, while in office, think that they are untouchable and invisible, hence they put their families and countries in serious problems. For example, the late president Saddam Hussein and Muammar Gaddafi, just to mention a few. They never thought they would be removed from their false security, let alone be killed. I can remember when Field Marshal Idi Amin was in power in Uganda. The demons that took hold of those people made them believe that they were semi-gods. An individual who is seriously on drugs feels he or she is on top of the world, feeling untouchable, which is a false sense of security. When the effect of the drugs wears out, they begin to feel the pain of emptiness, and at that point, the members of the family are affected also. The same goes for any dictator. While in power, everything looks wonderful—the fame, publicity, power, and being in control of the wealth of the nation. But whenever the inevitability happens as a result of a war, overthrownment, invasion or death of the dictator, the members of the family die along with them. In the past, there were countries who would give a dictator a safe haven in their countries, but very few countries are prepared to do so in the twenty-first century.

We shall be going into the main reason for this book; that is why it is dedicated to all the children of all races, both dead and alive, who have suffered in one way or the other.

CHAPTER 2

What God Said about Children

Let's just look over a few quotations and see how the Almighty God loves and how He wants parents to treat their children.

When a woman is pregnant, some have bad morning sicknesses, while others may have other symptoms, but as soon as the babies are born, all the pain is forgotten and joy comes in (John 16:21). And that child begins to receive attention from grandparents and so on.

The Bible goes on to say that children are the heritage of God and He is the one who blesses a womb to conceive a child. Jesus Christ warned his disciples not to prevent the little children from coming to Him that His kingdom belongs to them.

In Ephesians 6:4, Apostle Paul warned fathers not to hurt their children, instead to train, love, and bring them up properly in God's way. Why then should a father hurt, harm, let alone kill his or any other child? I came from a very big family, and God has blessed me with four wonderful children whom I cherish so much. How could I ever even think of harming them?

However, there are many parents who harm their children, and they would fall into one of the above categories mentioned. The government, police, general practitioners (GP), and social workers must do more in order to protect the innocent children who need help. The government must put some measures in place so that the social workers do not abuse the powers given to them. In some cases, the social workers have been found to have taken children out of their homes instead of helping the parent who might be going through a difficulty that is not detrimental to the life of the child.

When children are removed from their home suddenly without a serious reason, it affects the lives of those children directly or indirectly. While trying to do good, they end up hurting the parent and their children. If a child is in danger, especially if either of the parents or both are alcoholics, drug addicts, totally negligent, and the child is at risk, yes, the children should be removed and help should be offered to the parent immediately. Removing the children should not be used as punishment to victimize the parent.

We must bear in mind that mothers, whether sane or insane, conceived, carried, and bore those children. So there is an emotional attachment between a mother and a child. (Blood is thicker than water.) For example, a child who is well looked after by the parent and has never been smacked by the parent but is constantly inhaling the smoke from the cigarette of the parent is in danger of ill health. So there are several ways a child could be abused without any physical contact by an adult. On the cigarette packages, it is clearly stated that smoking can kill, but people still do it, and of course, it is a matter of choice. However, does the child have a choice? I don't think so. Could you imagine children choosing their parents based on whether or not they smoke, drink, or do drugs? So let's make our choices with the care of our children at heart.

Abused Children in a White Culture

As a minister of the gospel in Scotland, I work with children and parents four times a week in a church setting. Some of the children I worked with are now grown men and women, since I have been living and pastoring in Scotland for twenty-eight years. My eldest son is twenty-four years old now, and there were some children who were older than him in church when he was born. In a white culture, many white children are being abused without anyone knowing, even the next-door neighbour. It is a hidden practice because even their friends could inform the authority anonymously. This being the case, the child can be suffering for years and, in some cases, may die without anyone finding out the true cause of the death.

However in an African or black culture, the abuse can be done openly and no one will report the abuse to anyone. In one case I dealt with in Scotland, it was so horrible that the only reason I did not report that case to the authority was that the girl in question was sixteen years old at the time and had left her parents and had started attending our church in Kirkcaldy. Before, she was living with her parents in another part of Scotland where the sexual abuse took place repeatedly by her father. She confided in me that her own father was sexually abusing her and that her mother was aware. Even in Africa, parents can beat their children, and relatives will not report such an action. One of our members and I would pray for this young lady every week, and one day, I told her that I was going to go to the police. She warned me that she would deny what had happened to her before the police. But I could see the effects of the years of the abuse on this young lady. She began to sniff glue, take drugs, and use alcohol. For about a year of coming to church, she began to respond positively, singing and helping in the church. At this time, she was living in the home of a church member. In that year, she was clean of drugs and alcohol but was smoking cigarettes, which I was pleased about, judging from where she was before. I tried to meet either of her parents, but she completely refused it and would no longer discuss anything to do with her parents. She started being overfriendly and wanted more than I could offer her. When she was denied that intimate closeness, she left the church for more than six months and moved out of the house of the church member she was staying with. One day, I received a call from a hospital where people with mental issues are checked in. She had given them my name to call. I went to visit her and told her that she did not belong in that mental institution. I asked her, 'What are you doing here?' She confessed to me that she was back on drugs with her boyfriend. My first reaction was to be angry, but then, my mind went back to the years of sexual abuse she suffered at the hands of her father. I prayed and read the Bible with her and left. A week later, I travelled to India on a mission trip. Four days into my trip, I called the church back in Scotland and was told that this beautiful eighteen-year-old lady had taken her own life. I shouted, 'Oh my God, why should this girl die at this age?' This was about twenty years ago. I began to wonder, why did I not go to the police and report her father? Why did I promise that I would not tell anyone? But if I would not have promised, she would not have told me what she shared with me. If I were faced with the same situation again, I know better what to do.

I believe strongly also in ministerial confidentiality, but my wisdom now will prevail. May her soul rest in perfect peace. I did pray what the

Bible said in Galatians 6:7, 'Whatsoever a man soweth, that shall he also reap,' should happen to her parent.

Abuse will not stop because there are different kinds of individuals in the world. Just recently, we heard how over 1,300 children were sexually exploited in Rotherham, England, for over a sixteen-year period. Where were the social workers and the police? Majority of those children abused may never recover completely. The young lady I described previously left the house where the sexual abuse was taking place but was never the same, which was why she ended up in the mental hospital and eventually took her own life. In the case of Rotherham, England, for the authorities not to have detected this for sixteen years is unpardonable. When evil spirits take hold of a person, he or she becomes a tool of destruction and would not care who the victims are. The victims could be little babies, children in nursery or primary school, or children of high school age. A person who is possessed with evil spirits is not medically treatable, and no imprisonment can cure the situation. If a medical doctor in a hospital in Cambridge could sexually abuse over seven hundred children from as young as eight years old, this explains the magnitude of what we are talking about. If a child or a parent cannot trust a paediatrician, who else can they trust? This was a man who was fully possessed with evil spirits. *The report said that this doctor had carried examinations on children purely for his own sexual gratification.* How do you cure such a doctor? Where were the police and the social workers?

In our world of high-tech revolution, a possessed person does not have to dress shabbily, dirty, etc. No, he or she can be good-looking and influential. We must also be very careful so that we don't accuse an innocent person of an offence they did not and would not commit.

The most recent report in 2014 in Scotland reveals that child abuse is on the increase especially in my county of Fife. It was revealed that about eight hundred children were abused sexually within three years mostly in Fife and Glasgow. This revelation shows that there was a 40 per cent increase in child attacks in Scotland. Children must be educated about these attacks.

Since the figure revealed that among those who were attacked were mostly the sexually abused children between the ages of thirteen to fifteen years old, children must be warned about who they speak to on the Internet and at parties and the kind of signs to look for in an attacker. Also they must be warned about the use of alcohol, drugs, and so on. Prevention is better than cure. It is good for children to know where to access support, but it is better for the police in Scotland and the local authorities to put a plan in place to educate and instruct children before they become victims of government neglect.

It is vital to note that as these horrible cases are revealed, there may be still more hidden cases in different parts of the United Kingdom. If all the offenders were arrested and sent to prison, there may not be enough room in our prisons to accommodate them. Would prison sentence restore the dignity or the lives of the victims? Would the imprisonment change the lives of the offenders? This is where a little teaching about God's principles and the Bible should help. We shall talk about this just a bit more, because a reader may ask, 'How about the priests who have abused children?'

Abused Children in a Black Culture

I don't want to go into the history of slave trade. But the black man inherited his aggressive nature from the white man or the white slave master. It must be noted that God created the human beings in his likeness. Since this was the case, where did the wicked aggressiveness come from? Well, if you read the Bible in Genesis chapters 1 and 2, you see how God created man, while chapter 3 recorded when sin came into the world by disobedience.

The first murder ever is recorded in Genesis chapter 4. It tells how Cain killed his brother Abel. Let's get back to our topic, abuse in a black culture. Whether the black culture inherited their aggressiveness from the white slave masters or not, *it is not acceptable* in our modern society. In Africa, majority of the people don't believe that beating a child with an implement is an offense. This is why majority would not report such an incident to the authority. The man who is beating his child had also been subjected to such beating, if not worse. So he does not think that it is an offence, and no one would report any such thing to the authorities. The person in authority also could be doing the same things at home. Civilization has brought a bit of light into educating the back community, especially in the western world, that beating a child needlessly is wrong and barbaric.

In the olden days, African men tend to beat their wives for the slightest arguments, and no one would call it an abuse or an assault. Instead it was seen as a corrective measure for the misbehaving. Things have changed a great deal, but while the beating of wives has dwindled drastically, the beating of the children is still there. But it is very wrong to brand every black man or woman as a child beater or a molester.

Many black couples, rich or poor, Christian or non-Christian, have realized that if you love your children, you call them prince, princess, honey, sugar, etc., and you treasure them, not beat, hurt, harm, or kill them. There is a time and place for discipline; we shall look at this in a later chapter. As a black man, a minister of the Gospel, and a father, I know that a misbehaving child must be disciplined as a corrective measure and not as a punishment. For example, I will spank my child with my hands to correct him or her after warning him or her twice. The third time, they will get it. It will not harm a child. We are living in a society where many children have turned into something we see in a horror film. How can we have a peaceful and law-abiding society? These children will grow up to be youths then adults and, ultimately, our leaders. If they are undisciplined, we will be sitting on a time bomb, and by then, many will be moms and dads.

Have you wondered what would make a man wake up one morning and kill his wife? boyfriends kill their girlfriends? a mother with a knife kill her children and with no conscience whatsoever? children kill parents so as to inherit their possessions? I will tell you why these evil actions take place.

Proverbs 22:6

This biblical quotation says, 'Train up a child in the way he should go: and when he is old, he will not depart from it.' My friends, it does not matter if you believe in the Bible or not; this verse is true. You may say, 'I don't believe in the Bible, men wrote it.' Yes, holy men who were inspired by God. Okay, do we respect and obey the constitution? It was not written by God but by men. But we still obey and uphold it. Why do we respect and obey the police? They are human, and some of them are not so good, but we must respect what they represent.

We must then carefully examine the word *train*. We train dogs, horses, and military men and women who fight on our behalf. So why should a child not be trained to behave, to be respectful, and to know how to speak both at home and in public?

A British military person in training does not do what he or she likes. Instead he or she is told when to sleep, wake up, eat, go for a run, and so on. They are not even allowed to contact family members whenever they like; no, only on certain times and in an emergency. That is training. If you train someone well, you will reap the reward. Football managers train their players hard so as to get them to be fit and to get the best out of them. You don't have to be a church minister in order to believe the above verse from the Bible. A cow cannot breed a lion. Cow breeds cow, and lion breeds lion. You cannot give someone what you don't have. If you are an undisciplined parent, you cannot bring up a disciplined child. It surprises me when I see parents trying to correct their children in public for swearing, while at home they swear uncontrollably.

Black men can harm their children not even by touching them but by abandonment. You can seriously harm a child for life by simply abandoning a child. As a minister of the gospel and the founder of four churches, I am faced with children being abandoned by their fathers. We have taken full responsibility of their feeding, housing, clothing, and education. These are innocent children brought into this world by two adults and left to suffer either because Mom and Dad did not like each other anymore or in a case of a bad divorce. Whatever two adults decide to do with their lives, the children should not suffer as a result of that. I believe that children are blessings from God if we love and train them. They can also be a curse if we don't love and train them. A parent will reap whatever they sow into a child when that child is very young. It may be painful in the beginning, but it will be gainful in the end. So, parent, whether you are black or white or whatever colour, race, or creed you are, love, train, and sacrifice for your children, and you will not live in sorrow nor will you regret it.

As said earlier, it is only a man or a woman who is possessed who would harm or assault an innocent child or kill someone for whatever reason. I remember preaching in Lewiston, Idaho State, in America. After service, a tall man wanted to talk with me. As I sat down next to him, I thought he wanted to ask a question concerning my sermon. But he asked me if God could ever forgive his sins. I said yes, that God is always eager to forgive if we repent. He began to narrate the story that follows:

> My name is so-and-so. I used to listen to rock music day and night. The lyrics of one of the songs that I liked used to talk about killing someone. So one day, I heard a voice speaking to me to kill my best friend. I tried to ignore that voice, but it persisted, and finally, I called my best friend on his phone and invited him for a drive with my car. I drove him to an

alleyway, shot him with my gun, and set the car on fire. Then I called the police.

Every hair on my body stood as I was listening to this man.

He took a very deep breath, and I read a Bible scripture to him. I told him that God, through the death of Jesus Christ, would forgive him; however, there are consequences to our actions. I did not ask him in which state this crime had occurred, but he had already served his sentence. However, he could not sleep at night. Every time he would try to sleep, he would hear the voice of his friend. Though he had become a Christian while in prison, he could not have peace. He was on prescription medication. A year after our meeting, I went back to preach in Idaho. This time he came to meet me in Clarkston, Washington, at the house of my friends where I was staying. He said that he was seeing the face of his friend whom he had killed. Based on the Bible, I assured him that God had forgiven him after we had prayed together. However, he was still facing the consequences of his actions. Sad to say, two years later, he died. I remembered this story when I was reading an article from the *Daily Record* newspaper of 12 August 2014 about a woman who had told her doctor that she had stabbed her friend twenty-nine times to death because she had heard voices.

Is hearing voices the reason for harming someone, let alone killing them? Not at all. The reason for the abnormality of the mind should not even be accepted in any case of murder. Especially for the fact that the victims are not there to speak for themselves. Some people would use the loopholes in the law to escape stiffer sentences if that is not changed yet. I strongly recommend the law experts to seriously look into these cases and propose either an amendment to the existing law or a new law to be brought into place in order to avoid innocent people from being punished and the offenders to go free and for the lives of the vulnerable to be protected.

CHAPTER 3

Is It Wrong to Discipline Our Children?

What is discipline?

Discipline is instruction, correction, and training, which means you instruct and train to correct one's character. When you love a child or someone, you want the best for them. Discipline can sometimes include spanking a child on the hand or bottom without an implement. Do not slap the face, head, or anywhere else.

Proverbs 13:24 says if you don't correct your children, how can you say you love them? 'He who spares the rod hates his son, but he who loves him will discipline him.' In our house, we discipline our children if they are disobedient to the instructions or authority. They should be told what they did, why they are being disciplined, and why they should obey their parents or authority. If a child is not taught to obey at home, that child will not obey outside the home. 'Charity begins at home.' I have used dialogue, denied them something they like, and used spanking as a corrective measure, because I love them.

What is punishment?

Punishment is slightly different from discipline. Punishment is what I get after the offence. Even in the court of law, a person gets a form of punishment after he is convicted, not before. In some cases, that punishment does not correct that person. For example, I know a man who used to break into cars and homes, and he has been to prison at least six times for committing the same offence. Whenever he comes out of a prison, he is worse than when he went in. Finally I traced his behaviour to his childhood. I brought him to my office, went to his home, and realized that he was spoiled and untrained as a child at home. 'Train a child when he is young; when he is older he will not rebel against authority.' This man has seven children from five different ladies and is not responsible for any one of the children. He had become a drug addict. Is this the kind of role model we want for our children? You answer that question.

I know that this man had potential, and he told me one day that he did not want any of his children to be like him. He wanted to justify his behaviour one day and said to me, 'Pastor, I stole money from someone so I could get a Christmas gift for my children.' I rebuked him sharply. I told him that in the United Kingdom you don't need to steal in order to provide basic things for your children. Parents are paid or given child benefit and some allowances, which you would not get in Africa. You could save every month and buy presents for your children. Children need love and care, not presents. Some parents have spoiled their children by showering them with expensive presents, and they are abusive to the teachers, and the teachers can't do anything due to court cases or being charged for assault. The children grow up being told that they can report their parents or teachers if they are punished. Could you imagine what our society would be like if we don't have the police or courthouses? It would be hell on earth.

Consistency in Discipline

A Christian parent should know that your word should be your bond. Many parents lie to their children, and they wonder why their children are liars. You tell your child something, and you don't keep to your word. You make a promise to them, and you know you had no intentions of keeping your word. For example, if you warn your child that if he swore again in your presence, he would go to his room. If he does it again and again and you do not send him to his room, you are training him not to keep his word, and he will disrespect you because you cannot keep your word. Children can detect that quick. These kinds of children are those who would not want to do what the teachers say. The teacher would be talking to a child as if he were talking to a wall. In my time in primary school, if I was to be disobedient and unruly at school, my teacher had the God- and parent-given power to punish me. I would never do the same thing in that school again because I knew that I was wrong and my teacher was there to help me. Our parents would never go to school to ask the teacher why she/he had disciplined their child. Some parents would even discipline their children more for disgracing the family in public. This is why the older generation is more sensible and lives longer than the generation of today who starts learning how to smoke and drink from infancy. The time bomb is ticking and will explode if not defused carefully and in time.

Why Teach and Train

There is a difference in teaching and training. We teach our children when we tell them the right from wrong. We teach them to obey our authority, and when they do, we reward them. We teach them to obey the law of the land and the consequence of not obeying. As Christians, we teach them to obey the Word of God and tell them the reward that comes from obeying God's Word. If you are not a Christian, you can teach them to do unto others how they would want to be treated.

Training

We train a child when we help them to do something that is right. As we train them, we help shape their character. Younger children don't have self-belief to do what they need to do. We must train by example so that we make them do it. For example, 'Joseph, go and brush your teeth.' In order to make him do it, I would have to go into the bathroom with him and show him how to hold a brush and how to put toothpaste on a brush. I must train him to do that by brushing my own so that he can watch me do mine. Or 'Jessica, please go and tidy your toys.' I have to show her how to do it and where to put the toys. This is training. In the military service, the commander or the trainer who is to show a soldier how to shoot a gun must first teach the soldier what kind of gun he would be using. The name of the gun before the actual training, how to hold it, and how to shoot. You can see that teaching and training can go hand in hand. Another good example is a football player. No matter how talented that player may be, he must be taught and trained.

I played a little bit of football in Kirkcaldy, Scotland. Our manager would make us run and jump regardless of the weather. He decided who would play for him. Do—if you wanted to play, you had to do what he said. He decided the method he wanted to use in order to get the best out of his players. Do you know that even when the weather was very cold, he would stand out there watching? He would not go inside the house and tell us to get on with it. No, he stayed and watched who was following the rule and who was not. We have read in papers where professional football players were fined heavily for coming to training late or for not coming at all. Some of them are trained concerning their diets—what to eat and drink. Why are all these necessary to the big clubs? Because the clubs have invested a huge amount of money on the players, and they want a return by the players being among the best or the best in their profession. I have noticed also that when these players retire from active training and playing, their bodies begin to change, and some of their lifestyles are affected. Some become alcoholics, drug addicts, or out of shape, simply because they are no longer following the pattern of training they are used to. Some children beat their parents and grandparents. Once we miss the opportunity to teach and train them, it becomes too late. Why would your children want to go to church when they have never seen you go to church? Why would they want to pray if they have never seen you pray? If they don't learn from us, they will learn from somebody else, and that may be very destructive. If we are not a positive example for them, the world is full of negative examples for them.

Parents, stuffing your children with sweets is not training. You are laying a foundation for future health issues and creating more jobs for the dentist. Buying the latest, most expensive toys, phones, tablets, and laptops is not training. Many children have contacted loads of influences through these gadgets in their bedrooms without venturing out of their houses. I was so impressed with the Scottish *Daily Record* article on 15 September 2014 about Rod Stewart, his wife Penny Lancaster, and their children. They are wealthy parents who can afford to buy anything for their children, but they said that their eight-year-old son is not allowed a cell phone or a computer and cannot spend more than £20 on a toy. She said that as a good mother, she doesn't want her children to become spoiled brats. Her son is restricted to thirty minutes on the tablet each day. She taught her son to give away his birthday money to charity. She also said that she would try to teach him the value of money. She knows when to say no to the children and told them what they could and could not spend on their children. Parents, that's training as regards to materialism. This is not a matter of whether or not they are able to afford something for their children. The fact is that they can afford it, but they don't need it. Keep it up, Mrs Stewart! You are preparing a good leader of tomorrow for our country.

CHAPTER 4

Is the United Kingdom a Christian Nation?

'They will be my people and I will be their God' (Jeremiah 32:38). 'When the righteous rule, the people rejoice' (Proverbs 29:2). Can a man claim to be a student of a school if he does not attend physically or receive lectures online from that school? Can a man claim to be an employee of a firm if he does not work for that firm? You cannot claim to be Christian if you don't go to church, study or read the Bible, pray to God in the name of Jesus Christ, and more importantly, accept Christ as your Lord and Saviour. Just because you were born into a Christian home does not make you a Christian. If you go into a church building once or twice a year, does it make you a Christian? No. If I am employed as a cleaner at 10 Downing Street, does that make me a member of the prime minister's family? No. The United Kingdom was once a Christian nation but not anymore. Statistics of those who attend regular church services would affirm this. If parents did not take their children to church in their infancy, how do they expect them to continue in their adulthood?

The nation has abandoned God, who made the kingdom great. Many of our laws in this country are against the Word of God. For example, we passed the law to allow two females and two males to marry each other as a couple. This is directly in disobedience to the Bible. Even some pagan nations do not allow these practices. I am not against two consenting adults who have chosen their lifestyle, but the country does not and should not make it a law. If this is the case, why don't our lawmakers make it a law for the Bible to be taught in schools all over the country?

However, the Bible is used as a means of taking an oath in our courts. The Bible says that there are serious consequences for a nation that turns his heart away from their God. 'If that nation, against whom I have pronounced, turn from their evil, I will repent of the evil that I thought to do unto them' (Jeremiah 18:8).

The nation has turned to wickedness because the Great Britain that sent out godly men and women as missionaries all over the world is now worshipping a different god. Our youths are not interested in God because their parents were ungodly, wild, valiant, unlawful, and were experts in fraud who would not obey the authority.

How many prison buildings are we going to build that would contain the offenders? The one thing that represents God, e.g. the church, is out of fashion, and what represents the devil, such as violence, drunkenness, drug abuse, and brothels, is on the increase. *I see a time bomb ticking in the United Kingdom.* A country that was once abundantly blessed by God, a country that once colonized the world, once the safest nation on earth, is now afraid of her own children bringing her down. May God Almighty, who is merciful, have mercy on us in this nation.

Vendetta, Victimization, and Viciousness from Stirlingshire Social Work

The new laws came into force in England and Wales on Saturday, 29 March 2014, allowing same-sex marriages. I thought I was living in a democratic society. So I decided to air my personal opinion based on the Bible quotations in Leviticus 18:22 and Leviticus 20:13, which forbade same-sex marriages. I, as a minister, do not, cannot, and will not hate any homosexual couple. We have had them in our church before. However, I am 100 per cent against their behaviour and lifestyle. Am I not entitled to that? Not everyone approves of my lifestyle, and they are entitled to their opinions. But no one is entitled to either criticize, disapprove, or victimize me based on the colour of my skin. This is how God Almighty created me, and I will not change anything from it.

So on Monday, 31 March 2014, an interview I gave was published in the Scottish *Daily Record* with the caption 'It's Pastor Joke'. I then travelled to Nigeria on the sixth of April to visit our churches, Bible school, and orphanage. I was out of the country until 23 April 2014. While I was in Nigeria, Africa, preaching and helping to feed the hungry people, I did not know that some of those who had read the newspaper publications (e.g. social workers and our lady's head teacher) were planning against me back in Scotland. When I arrived in Scotland on the twenty-third of April, I had not even unpacked my bags; on the twenty-fourth, I got a call from my wife, who had gone to our children's school to pick them but was refused. She was told by the social worker from the Stirlingshire council that she was accused of assaulting our son. I said, 'Okay, I will come and pick them up,' but she passed her phone to the social worker, who then said that I was also accused, so I could not come to pick our children. When I heard our daughter's voice crying on the phone for me to come, I knew at that moment that the devil was after me. I requested the phone to be given to our daughter; I calmed her down and reassured her that everything would be okay. I went into prayers and committed the wicked plan of the devil into God's hands. From 3.30 p.m., I did not hear anything from my wife, our children, the school, or the social worker until 11.30 p.m. at night.

The social worker told me that I was needed for questioning at the Stirlingshire police station. I knew that my wife was already in a police cell and our ten- and eight-year-old children were already placed with a lesbian couple as their foster care. The vendetta had already begun less than seven hours after I had spoken to the social worker at 3.30 p.m. By this time, I was ready, both spiritually and otherwise, for this case. I was ready to go to prison for our children. By the time I had contacted my lawyer, it was late. So the next day, Friday, 25 April 2014, I drove myself to the Stirlingshire Police Station. I had the name and the number of the detective to contact, but when I had arrived there, she was not in the office. The officer I spoke with asked me what kind of a car I had driven down with. I told her. She then asked for the plate number. After I gave the plate number, she then asked me to drive the car and park it inside the station. I already knew that I would be detained. I grew up in a force family. My late father was a police officer, my three uncles were police officers, my first cousin is a retired police commissioner, another cousin is a retired deputy inspector general of police, and my other uncle was a retired army colonel. From experience, I knew from my dad that the law is made for the offenders and you are innocent until proven guilty.

At the Stirling Police Station

As I was parking my car, a police officer told me where to park. As soon as we went inside, I was read my rights as 'Whatever you say . . .' She took me to the counter, collected my key so that she could search my car, which she did and found nothing. I was booked into my 'five-star hotel police cell' in Stirling. I have heard some very bad things about police officers in cases like this, but my experience was very good.

I went into the cell. Compared with the cells in Africa, this was indeed a super 'five-star hotel prison cell.' I was given clean blankets and a pillow, wow. I was in the cell for about nine hours. I was offered food, tea, and water; I declined all the offers. I prayed all through my stay in there. The police kept coming to ask me if I was okay. I had not been told yet what offence I had committed or where my family was. However, after three hours, I was told that the social worker wanted to talk with me. I was brought out of the cell into a room where two social workers were waiting.

They told me that my son had told the school head teacher that I had beaten him with a metal cane. I immediately said to them that my son had not said it and that it was not true. By then I was very angry at the social work system and the school for fabricating a story against me. They lied to me that our children were settled with a nice couple and that we would see them soon, while in fact our children had been crying for their parents. They came with a form for me to fill so that our children could be examined by a doctor, which I filled and signed, since I had nothing to fear.

I was taken back to my executive cell, and I continued my prayers more intensely after I had been told what I was being accused of. A few hours later, I was brought out for interview by a female police officer and a male detective. I was reminded that whatever I said would be used as evidence against me in court if need be. Both video and audio tapes were rolling as I was being questioned. I told the truth, the whole truth, and nothing but the truth, and God whom I serve helped me. The police reiterated what the social worker had said: that our son had said that I beat him with a 'metal cane in April 2014'. I told the police that the last time I had seen our children Joseph and Jessica was in March because I had travelled to Africa on a mission. All my children are very well behaved; they were brought up in a Christian way. I answered all the questions accordingly.

Spare the Rod and Spoil the Child (Proverbs 13:24)

The Bible says, 'If you spare the rod, you will spoil your son. But if you love him, you will chastise him.' So the police quoted the above Bible verse to me, that my son had said that we had used it to justify the punishment. I told the officer that as a minister, I have preached from so many biblical verses including the above one, but never to justify any punishment. I am blessed with four wonderful children: Joel, Jethro, Joseph, and Jessica. The first two are from my first marriage. If the above verse is used in my house to justify punishment, then my older children would have been conversant with that scripture. When they heard what I was being accused of, they were horrified, to say the least. I believed that the head teacher of the school, who invited our son into her office concerning a different case that happened in school, told my son to say something and called the social worker without asking us anything. She knew I had travelled but did not know I was back from Africa.

On that Saturday, 29 March 2014, in our church building, our children were practising songs while I was upstairs in my office preparing my sermon. I heard a noise in the sanctuary downstairs. When I came down, they were running around inside playing. I called them together and reminded them that this was a house of God and not to do that but to continue with the practice of songs. As usual they answered, 'Yes, Daddy.' I went back to my office, and after thirty minutes, I heard a big bang downstairs. I rushed down thinking that someone had fallen. I was shocked to see them fighting and pushing around the chairs. So I took a small cardboard paper, folded it, and spanked both of them and took them upstairs. They were warned never to fight and not to run around inside the sanctuary. I gave them an example that if we went to 10 Downing Street, the official home of our prime minister, would they be allowed to run around and fight? They said no and apologized. After that, we went to the park and jumped on the trampoline. I know it was in March because I was away, and no cane, certainly not any metal, was used in disciplining them. I was glad the police confirmed that the children said that it was the only time it had happened, bearing in mind that they were ten and eight years old at the time. The police detective read the interviews she had with our children about how they were missing us and wanted to see us. The black children, who had never been separated from their parents since they were born, would be removed straight from their school and be placed into a white lesbian foster care home. Could you imagine the trauma? Was that action for the best interest of the children? Was the law fair to our children? Was this not a well-planned vendetta? I leave the answers to you, the reader. After all the interrogations, I duly signed my statement and was discharged without any charges. Another two male detectives went with me to my office and house to search for a metal cane but found nothing.

CHAPTER 5

The Children's Hearing

The case referred to the children's hearing panel to decide the case of assault against us. On 2 May 2014, we appeared at the hearing and were given the written narrative, all the offences we were supposed to have committed against our children. On the list were eight charges, which we denied. We answered no to all the charges. For instance, how could I agree that I had beaten my children with a metal cane in April when I did not do it? I said, 'Not guilty' and asked the panel to refer it to the Stirling sheriff court.

By then, we had not heard nor seen our children. In that hearing, it was agreed that we should see them for one hour under supervision in one of the rooms in a high school in Stirling. The next day, after school, our children were brought into the room. I can't describe their fear. They jumped on us shaking, crying, and screaming. After ten days, they smelled; they had only had a shower twice in ten days. Our children take a bath every day and sometimes twice a day. My heart was hurt when they told us that the couple they were staying with were lesbians. That was when we knew. The detective, the school, and the social worker did not want to tell us that the couple was a lesbian couple. Our children are very intelligent. They know what the Bible says. When the one hour was over, the crying increased. They were telling us not to allow them to be taken back to that house. I cannot write in this book what was going through my mind. But I wished that I had supernatural powers to close my eyes and see them transported to Nigeria. We told them that we would win this case, but that was not what they wanted to hear. They wanted to return home to their parents. I did not sleep for days. I kept hearing our children's screaming and was determined to fight the case to the end.

The children's hearing was an ongoing thing. Every two weeks, we had to appear to hear from the social worker, the head teacher, and the foster care as to how our children were coping both in school and at the foster home. I saw how someone in a position of authority can live constantly. We were told that our children were settling fine both at school and with the foster care.

The children's panel kept adjourning the hearing from week to week, and our time for seeing the children was changed to twice a week for one hour.

Stirlingshire Social Worker

When the social worker saw that we were not accepting their accusations against us, our case was classified a long time, and a new social worker who would continue with the case was introduced to us. Then a safe guarder was also appointed. I was not expecting the new social worker to be fair or be favourable to us. She would have to obey the instructions of her bosses. I never envisaged that children would be placed in a foster care from 24 April until 12 September 2014. I could have volunteered to go to prison for them to be at home.

The social worker and the head teacher would come to the children's hearing and give reports about our children. And when we would meet them during our weekly visit, they would be shocked to hear from us what had been reported by these individuals. The social worker did not care that our children had a right to their faith. The children, who had never missed a single church service since they were born, were denied going to church from twenty-fourth of April until the twelfth of September. Was their duty not for the interest of the children? Why was it that adequate plans were not made for them to go to church? I told the social worker that they had to go to church, read their Bibles, and pray. However, I knew that these things would never happen once we found out whom they were staying with.

Was there no other foster care couple in Stirling where our children could have been taken to? There were other couples, but the Stirling social worker chose the lesbian couple in order to personally get at me because of my view about homosexuality. My views have not and will not change.

Everyone is entitled to theirs, but why subject our children to unnecessary pain in a case where there was no abuse or assault? We don't drink, we don't smoke, and we don't use any kind of drugs. Our children have never heard a swear word at home or seen us fight. Why then did they pick us? Our children heard the couple they were staying with swear at each other. The social worker placed our children in a home that was not healthy for them. They know my job and my stance. Our children were placed in a home in the town of Cowie in Stirlingshire, and on two occasions that the couple had gone on a vacation, our children were moved to stay with another foster couple, a man and a woman in the town of Doune in Stirlingshire. Why were our children not placed with this couple in the first place? Our children spent part of their summer holiday with the second couple.

The whole summer, while other children were spending the holidays with their families, ours were being transferred from stranger to stranger. Their head teacher went on holiday with her family, the social worker went on a holiday with her family, and the foster care went to Canada to visit their children, while ours were kept against their wishes in a strange home. Our children had to eat their favourite African dishes when we would come to visit them at a strange place. Our daughter's hair had to be plaited during our supervised visit. We had to give our son a haircut while being supervised at a strange place. We kept reassuring them that this was a trial we had to overcome so that other innocent families would not have to go through the same. At the end of every visit, we would pray together before we parted company. They started to feel stronger and did not want to ever trust or speak to any male or female white person. They became bitter, and we had to tell them that their anger was justifiable, but we would not be bitter. As Christians, we are not and should not be bitter against anyone, but we must pray for justice.

Case Referred to the Sheriff Court

The children panel concluded and referred the case to court. We were very happy, and our children were happy also. We believe in the judicial system of the country. We knew that if our children would ever have any hope of coming home, the court would have to decide that. And we were right. The social worker, the head teacher, the safe guarder, and the foster care were all saying the same thing: that although our children wanted to come home, it was not yet the time. How can it be that the children wanted to come home at once, but these people were denying them their human rights? We were happy that the sheriff had seen the children and felt that it was unfortunate that they had been kept away for this long. On 12 September 2014, he ordered that our children be released immediately. It further supports my belief about the judicial system of the country. The social worker was still preparing a timetable of our contact visit until October while the children came home on the twelfth of September.

Like I had stated in the previous chapters, some children have been in danger, and many have, and still may be, suffering in certain homes all over the land. There must be measures in place to differentiate parents and families. Even in courts sometimes, before someone is sentenced, a background check is recommended. In our case, I was told on the phone that I could not come to collect our children from school. A few hours later, they were placed in care because we found out later that one of the foster care lesbian ladies worked at the school. So it was easy to place our kids in their care. I would not wish any decent and innocent family to go through what we went through, but I would willingly go to the police cell again so that another family would not suffer this. In the next chapter, we will discuss how to protect our children from abduction and assault.

CHAPTER 6

Protecting Children from Abduction and Assault

Child assault and abduction is not a new thing in the world. It has been in existence since wickedness and slavery began. Every evil thing that is being perpetuated on earth originated from Satan. This book is written in order to help us live godly, peaceful, and civilized lives; therefore, I will not glorify evil by dwelling in it. In the Bible, you will find out that abuse, assault, and wickedness took place. The Bible warns us to have anything to do with works of darkness; instead, to expose and stand against it (Ephesians 5:11–12). My intention is not to force the reader to become a Christian or to start going to church, but it is to alert us about the dangers that our children face and also to prepare them to not only to identify the dangers but also how to avoid them. A parent who is ignorant to these dangers should be ready for the sorrow that will come. In our world today, parents must be willing to sacrifice time, and they also need to talk with their children. This is why education is so vital today more than ever. An informed parent will not be easily misinformed.

For instance, many years ago majority of the white community did not want to believe or accept that there is even a word called *racism*. A racist would not believe that he or she was one. Well-educated people, Christians, and wealthy were, in some cases, racist. Someone who is racist would not report or do anything if he saw a child or anyone of another colour being assaulted or abducted. It goes into the blood of the society, and it has become a cancer that is spreading. This was why I asked the one-billion-pound question: 'Is United Kingdom a Christian nation?' If we are, then we should know that God created every human being regardless of their colour. We are also given a commandment to love one another.

Hatred is racism. If you hate a person so much that you mock, insult, and discriminate against him/her, you are a racist and you need some serious help. As I travel all over to spread the good news of the love of Jesus Christ, I meet people who claim that they are not racist. But when I would ask them if they would allow or support their children to marry a person of another colour, they would say no. Some would say it is up to their children. Even amongst black communities, some tribes would never permit their children to marry someone from another tribe. It is very sad that wickedness is so deep-rooted into our society by the devil.

Well, today it is no longer hidden. Why is our government and football governing body FIFA campaigning against this evil? Because it is happening in the offices, schools, universities, football stadiums, and unfortunately, in the church. Can I say it now again? Racism can *never* be eradicated. It may be reduced but cannot be removed. If I were a racist, I would teach my children to be one, and they will teach theirs, and so it will go on. In sports, some children support a team because their father or grandfather supports that same team. Scotland and England—why do you think that these two blessed nations hate each other? Who taught a little primary school child not to support each other's teams, even when they are *not* playing against each other? A time bomb is ticking in the UK. The 18 September 2014 Scottish referendum was an example of what I am saying, and it will just allow this sleeping monster to lie, but I would want every parent to judge their conscience.

What Is Child Abuse or Assault?

What some people consider as abuse others think is normal. That is why many turn a blind eye when they see abuse, while others would report it even if it was a normal chastisement or correction due to malicious reasons. So what is child abuse? Abuse is any physical, verbal, sexual, or emotional mistreatment of a child that is motivated by anger or trickery. One can trick a child into false love while abusing them. So abuse can happen when an adult does what he considers to be good for himself even though it hurts the child. He reacts out of his own selfish interest rather than in the child's best interest. In some cases, children who were abused often grow up to abuse their own children. They treat their kids the same way they were treated.

Every parent or guardian, at one point, feels angry and frustrated when their children disobey, insult, defy, or talk back to them. Sometimes we are tired after a long day's work, and we just want them to do everything they are asked to do. And if they don't, we snap and sometimes go out of control. We are human, but so are they. If we were bad with anger before becoming a Christian, our character or nature just doesn't disappear overnight. It takes time; it is a gradual process until we are completely changed. This is why praying, reading the Bible, and church attendance are vital. This is why self-control is very important. God also uses people to make us change, such as our doctors, church ministers, counsellors, and other professionals. That is why we are recommended anger management and addiction clinics.

Abduction and Molestation

Children want to feel safe in the hands of their parents. I would say it is their God-given right. I always felt very safe in the company of my parents as a child. You feel so protected as if nothing can harm you. I noticed that with my children also. Many years ago, the parents' job was to watch their kids from injuring themselves in the playground and at home. But added to the parents' responsibilities now are protecting the children from possible molestation and abduction. Our eyes are always watching out to know where they are. If they are younger children, we make sure that we can see them as they play. If they are older, we call, email, and text them to check on them. Many parents are naive as to the subtle and divisive ways child molesters and abductors think and operate. Some parents think and wish that it will not happen to them. Do not think that it would not happen to you; instead, start by teaching them to say no to strangers and let them know the dangers. Teach them not to accept gifts, sweets, or money or sit on the lap of someone you don't approve of, whether in school, playground, or at church. As Christian parents, we pray with our children for God, who sees and knows all things, to protect them.

Because of the dangers of this generation, we have CCTV cameras almost everywhere imaginable: at the airports, streets, schools, shopping malls, you name it. You will find camera and law enforcement people almost everywhere, even at sports stadiums. All these measures are for our protection.

If you suspect, sport or see your child or any other being molested or abducted, call the police, and they will connect or contact the appropriate authority. If it is your child, you have the right to see the doctor for check-up and advice; if it is someone else's child, the police will know what to do. Note the date, time, and the name of the police officer you reported the case to in case there is a conflict of interest with the suspects and no further action is taken. The same way a church minister has friends and social workers, police have friends also. There have been cases where the police, social workers, politicians, priests, and ministers have molested children. If we love those children, we will do the right thing.

These are some ways parents endanger their children:

a. Ephesians 6:1–3

'Children, obey your parents in the Lord, for this is right. Honour your father and mother, which is the first commandment with promise: that it may be well with you and you may live long on the earth.'

If an adult tells you to do something, you should do it. While it is good for them to be taught to obey and respect authority, they must know that they have the right to disobey any authority that is being misused. He/she must be taught that if the teacher, pastor, doctor, family member, or anybody wants to touch him/ her in a way that makes them feel uncomfortable or is asked to do something that feels wrong, they must say a big no and tell their parents—they won't get in trouble.

b. Parents, please listen to your children.

If you train them well, you will know when and if they are lying. You don't want your children to accuse someone wrongly and that could destroy that person's life. You must know them, ask them questions, and listen to their body language; find out who their friends are and the kind of homes they come from. Our son once told me that his football coach smokes 'something' in the minibus and that the coach's son swears just like his father.

That was the end of that football training and him playing in that team.

c. Parents, be your children's friends.

If the children see you as their friend, they will tell you anything. There are things about me that my friends know but my brothers don't know. We tend to open up to our friends. Have you told your friend something and asked them not to tell anybody? Yes, but you forgot that your friend also has his/her best friends. Make your kids know that they can talk about anything with you. When we were growing up, we did not discuss any sexual issues with our dads; that was part of culture also. But it must change in this century. A child who is not encouraged to discuss sexual issues or ask Mom and Dad sex-related questions may not be comfortable to tell them if they are being molested.

d. Parents, please hug your children.

Some parents are afraid that if they hug or cuddle with children, especially teenagers, that the children would be embarrassed in front of their friends or be assaulted of incest. Our children need kisses and hugs. If you know your child, you will know when they need your hugs or kisses. When our two- and ten-year-old children were forced into foster care, they missed our hugs and kisses so much that they would hug us and not let go. They would ask their mom to put bright-red lipstick kisses on the school jumpers and coats. At the end of every contact visit, we would carry them on our backs from the room to where the foster parents' or social worker's cars were parked. We would cuddle up together, sometimes on the couch covered with a duvet to watch TV together. Some children would feel rejected if parents stopped hugging or kissing or showing affection because they are growing older. Hugs must not stop even when the kisses stop due to their age. Molesters can spot symptoms of vulnerability. If child is withdrawn or depressed due to a feeling of rejection, that child could be a target for molesters.

Protect Your Children from Abduction

Children need the protection of adults, and they deserve our protection.

a. Watch your children closely at all times. Do not leave them alone in the car while you are shopping, don't leave them alone in the compound or in a public place, and always try to know where your children are.

b. Do not place your child's name on his or her schoolbooks and bags. If you do, it may give a potential abductor opportunity to know your child's name. A child who hears his or her name called by a stranger may engage in conversation with a stranger.

c. You don't have to be photogenic, but take several photos of your child both in school uniforms and casual clothes. It will help you if your child happens to be missing. Children who can speak and write should be taught emergency numbers, house addresses, full names of their parents, the town and the city where they live, and how to call the police.

d. Give the schoolteacher, the head teacher, or the principal the power to notify you, the parent, if your child did not report to the school. If you are a Christian, your church should inform you if your son or daughter who said they were going to a youth group did not show up.

e. You try to find out who their friends are and, subsequently, who their friends' parents are. Be careful how you allow your child to a sleep over at a friend's house. When you allow them for a sleepover, find out what they will be watching and doing. Some kids have access to strangers via social media in their bedrooms.

f. Finally you must pray for them and leave the rest to God, who knows what we don't know and sees what we don't see.

Some Signs of Sexual Abuse in Children

As parents, we need to be watchful of these signs in our child:

1. Appears to be withdrawn suddenly
2. Begins to do poorly in school and a sudden change in his/her class grade or result
3. A sudden change in appetite without being ill or sick
4. Becomes sexually promiscuous or provocative in the way he or she dresses
5. Engages in excessive and compulsive masturbation
6. Suddenly and unannounced runs away from home and will not tell the parent of their destination

CHAPTER 7

The Dangers of Drugs, Alcohol, and Tobacco

One of the biggest fears confronting families today is drug and alcohol abuse. This includes all the smoking, swallowing, sniffing, injecting, inhaling, chewing, and drinking substances that children pump into their bodies. We can abuse our own bodies by what we willingly pump into our bodies. Many of the reported rape cases are associated with alcohol and drug intake. Without mentioning any names, in our world, some gifted and talented footballers, singers, and movie stars have died prematurely due to drug and alcohol abuse. Yet the abuse of these substances is on the increase. Young children of high school age are constantly experimenting with the use of tobacco, alcohol, and drugs. It is not enough to ask the parents to educate children at home. How can a parent who consumes these substances teach their children how to abstain from such practices? Our governments are not doing enough to stop these merchants of death in our society. Our government should be passing the law to reduce, stop, or eradicate the abuse of drugs, alcohol, and tobacco, which is for the interest of the majority of the public. But the members of the parliament went ahead to pass the law for same-sex marriage, which is not of interest to the majority of the public. A man or woman under the influence of drugs, alcohol, and tobacco is a 'ticking time bomb', and that is why it must be taken seriously and be dealt with. Why can't our politicians debate and vote on something that is this dangerous? Is it the case of replaced priorities? The British Rape Crime Survey says that 24,000 women have been reported raped in 2014. This is an alarming figure, and majority of these cases are either drug- or alcohol-related or both.

What Can Parents Do?

a. Inform your children about the danger of drugs, alcohol, and tobacco. Advise them not to yield to peer pressure and that they should say no.

b. Teach them to respect authorities and at an early age to respect and believe God who created them.

c. Be consistent with your rules; there must be privileges to be lost if they experiment with these substances. Use a pop, football, or movie star as an example of its danger.

Let's be good examples of what we are teaching them. We cannot ask them not to take these substances if they see us consume them. Let it not be the case of the blind leading the blind. Our children should see us as their heroes. If we don't train or advise them, it will come back and hurt us. If your child kills someone or himself due to consuming any or all the above-mentioned substances, it will hurt you until death. An African adage says, 'Search for a missing black goat during the day, because at night you may not be able to see it.' It simply means that governments, schools, churches, mosques, media, and parents must keep emphasizing the dangers of drugs, alcohol, and tobacco abuse.

CHAPTER 8

Terrorism in the United Kingdom

The word *terror* means 'fear, to intimidate with fear, to terrorize people by intimidation'. Terrorism is getting what one wants in politics by using force or murder. A terrorist is a person or organization who uses violence and murder to propagate his or its agenda. With all these definitions in mind, one can see that the seed of terrorism is being sown in the United Kingdom. The government is partly to be blamed for the way the citizens of the country travel out to join the terrorist groups and return to harvest the seed of terror that has been sown. In the name of free speech, in the name of tolerance, and in the name of free religious beliefs, we have created a monster that is too big to kill and a fire that is too overspread to extinguish.

Religion is part of the problem but not Christianity. Religion is a man-made opinion and idea that is contrary to the teachings of the Holy Book, the Bible. In my opinion, some sections of the law should be amended. For example, freedom of speech. These words have been misused by the majority of the population. Young children in schools don't care about what they do to their teachers; they can insult their teachers because of freedom of speech. Anyone can talk or insult Her Majesty or the prime minister without being accountable because of the so-called freedom of speech. I think it should be changed to the freedom of insult. I don't have to insult my opponents in order to make my views known.

We say what happened during the September 2014 Scottish Referendum. Political opponents were abused verbally and physically in the United Kingdom, not in Africa or in the Middle East. A country that is known for her democracy was practicing *democrazy* in public, and our children were watching. If a young man or woman knows that if they travel out of the United Kingdom to any country to train in jihad or terror and return to fight their country, there must be a strong punishment that such person will think twice before engaging in such act. There is absolutely nothing the parents can do. Their children have unlimited and uncontrolled freedom given to them by the law. They have freedom of speech, freedom of association, and freedom of manufacturing whatever they want. In a world of technology, a schoolboy can be manufacturing a bomb in his bedroom or in his parents' garage or in garden sheds. When these things are made, they must be tested to the detriment of the public.

The man named Job in the Bible said, 'The thing I fear the most has happened to me' (Job 3:25). In the United Kingdom and United States, we are used to hearing that people's hands and limbs are cut off as a punishment for certain offences in some countries, and there is an outcry from human rights organizations. Then came the beheading of innocent people's heads, and the world was outraged about this barbarism and evil act. No one ever thought we would see heads beheaded in the United Kingdom and United States. What should this kind of behaviour teach us?

1. Do not give unlimited and uncontrolled power to a human being. If you do, don't complain when it's used.
2. Too much freedom is dangerous. If you free someone too much, he will dominate. If you free a lion in a zoo, people will die. If you free a wild dog, people will die. If you free a demon-possessed murderer from prison, people will die.
3. There must be checks and balances. I am not supporting dictatorship, never, but a law that can help a madman from being worse and a quite sane man from being taken advantage of.

A man-made government-allowed time bomb is inevitable if nothing is done by those who have the power to vote, who voted same-sex marriage into law in a supposedly Christian country. In October 2014, the Catholic Synod made up of cardinals voted against such practices being made part of Catholic law. The so-called law of inclusion and tolerance has caused so much trouble in our world. In law, the murderer is excluded from open or normal prison where minor offenders are kept. A patient with a serious disease is excluded from others with minor illnesses. Why doesn't the law of inclusion and tolerance extend to every part of human lives? Because it is dangerous. An African idiom says, 'Remove the fingers of the monkey in your pot of soup before it becomes a human's fingers.' It means our lawmakers who have a godly conscience should initiate a good, life-saving change now while it is possible before it becomes too costly, life-damaging, and impossible. Can you imagine what will happen in the UK if a terrorist, a racist, and a rapist at heart are elected into the houses of Commons and Holyrood?

God have mercy. I may have lived my life and finished my cause, but how about my children? I will not listen to anyone who is saying that it will not happen. It will happen in a country that has systematically removed God from its homes, schools, public places, and also from some church gatherings. You cannot love what you don't value. If you don't value your country, you can't love it. If you don't value your neighbours, you cannot love them, and if you don't value your Creator, you can neither love nor obey what he says. Ladies and gentlemen, terrorists are living in our midst, but they go about the streets like any other person until an opportunity presents itself, then they take it. You only know a racist when he or she manifests the act. But they go about like any other person doing their businesses. Someone can carry a banner with a sign Give Racism a Red Card while he himself is a racist.

I believe in democracy, but too much freedom allows people to take laws into their hands. Laws are made by humans and broken by humans. Animals don't make laws, and they don't break laws. For example, in the hands of butchers, knives are domestic tools, but in the hands of terrorists, they are lethal weapons.

The chief of police of Scotland made a comment recently, after the shooting in Paris, France, that the police would shoot a terrorist who would use any weapon, including a knife, to endanger the lives of the public. I agree totally with him as regards a terrorist. But how about a teenager who has never travelled out of the country and has never seen the websites of jihadists but is on drugs and is carrying a knife as a weapon in a public place? Should he be shot dead, being controlled by a substance?

The police may be shooting the future prime minister of United Kingdom to death. The government needs to start investing in the future of the leaders of tomorrow and ban those substances they use or consume, which are harmful to their health and are a time bomb in our country. Some people might argue that by doing so, you are denying one's freedom or human rights. The terrorists can claim that they have the right of freedom of speech, to own a weapon, to travel to any country that they wish, and to belong to any organization they like. Can Paris ever be the same again? I doubt it. The effects of 9/11 are still being felt all over the world. Our police and secret security agencies are doing fabulous jobs in tough circumstances. In some cases, they are putting their lives in danger in order to protect the public and safeguard our country. We, the public, can help the police by giving information about suspicious movements, alerting police of abandoned vehicles, luggage kept in unusual places, and comments made by individuals that may be of help to the police in tracking criminals. Criminals do not always wear masks. They look as normal as we are. So be vigilant.

CHAPTER 9

The Just and the Unjust Wars

May I declare that I am not writing this on behalf of any person, group, church, race, or country. This is my personal opinion, and anybody is welcome to criticize or disqualify my opinion. As a citizen of the free world, I am entitled to mine. There are wars that should be considered just and also some that are not. In my case of a war, there must be casualties. Many are killed, some are disabled for life, properties are destroyed, and in some cases, they cannot even be rebuilt. Even in the Bible, there were records of wars. For example, the Philistines against Israel with David versus Goliath and the Roman Empire versus the Jews.

Although some wars may be just, some are originated due to greed, selfishness, and wickedness. I believe that so many past wars could have been avoided if they were not out of greed or selfishness. I am an immature lay and complete novice in a military circle, but I will give a few examples of wars that could and should have been avoided.

Iraq War

I will agree that the late Saddam Hussein was a dictator. If you want to call him a wicked leader, I will also agree with that. If you choose to call him a madman, I will not disagree with that either. But even a mad person has a friend. Our government (the British government) did not explore every avenue before voting to go to war. Well, some people have blamed the former Prime Minister Rt. Hon. Tony Blair for taking Britain to war. In my opinion, every member of the parliament who voted for the invasion of Iraq has a bloodstain in his or her hands. Saddam Hussein had friends whom he could have listened to as a mediator; he allowed the United Nations entry to check the so-called chemical weapon site, but nothing was found. If the MPs voted because he had used such a weapon in the past, it should have been explained in the House of Commons, but that was not the case.

Britain went to war because it was supposed that Saddam Hussein had stocks of dangerous chemical weapons, which he was planning to release on to the public. As a result of the MPs' decision, thousands of people have died, both British and Iraqi, who should have been alive in 2014. If the MPs had voted no to war in Iraq, would Tony Blair have gone to war? No, he couldn't have. In 2014, the present prime minister, Rt. Hon. David Cameron, wanted the House of Commons to support his request to send troops and air strike to Syria. The members of parliament voted against it. Was he able to carry out his mission? No. He was not given the power by the MPs, but they gave Tony Blair the power, and he went into war. What good did the Iraq war do? I leave you to think before answering that question. Saddam has gone, but the war still rages. People are still dying; those who are alive are in fear of being driven out of their homes without being able to take any of their personal belongings. Who knows when it will end?

If the House of Commons had not voted against war in Syria, Britain would have been in a war as I write. Dead bodies of our soldiers would have been flying back home. One man said, 'A hero who is alive is better than a hero who is dead.' If the British government had tactically removed Saddam Hussein, dead or alive, with less casualty as in the case of what the American government did with Osama bin Laden, many people would have supported the move.

Dictators

I believe that there should be no room or hiding place for any dictator of any country. But I also strongly disagree that it is worth killing a dictator and killing thousands of innocent lives, causing many to be disabled and destroying the economy of the country. There is unemployment in countries that have not faced many kinds of wars, let alone a country that is in a war or has gone through war.

Libya

Before the war in Libya, President Gadhafi was a friend of many western countries. I know that when there is war, countries also use the opportunity to sell arms and all the other weapons of war. I am not against selling of arms from country to country that could be done for defence purposes. I believe also that President Gadhafi could have been alive in 2014 if proper negotiations by friends of both sides had been encouraged with patience. Many died in Libya, the economy got destroyed, and people suffered as a result of the war.

Is Libya better with Gadhafi or without? The country is ravaged with lives destroyed, and the war is still raging. Gadhafi was killed in 2011, but in 2015, the country that was booming in oil when he was alive is poorer, and people are fleeing the country as more deaths are recorded daily. The capital, Tripoli, as recorded by reporters, is unrecognizable, and the economy is worse than ever. As the saying goes, 'The enemy you know is better than the saint you don't know.' Libya may never be the same again.

Nigeria and Biafran War, 1967

This war was caused by greed and inequality. The Nigerian government at that time wanted to rule and control the wealth that God had placed in the country. Nigeria is a blessed and large nation that only a few individuals from one tribe wanted to control the nation. When the leaders of the factions could not agree, a meeting was arranged by the president of Ghana to settle the dispute between these faction leaders. It was reached on a mountaintop in Aburi/Ghana for confederation governance on 30 May 1967. On arriving in Nigeria, the Nigerian leader at that time refused to carry out the reached agreement in Ghana. The leader of the Igbo faction known as Biafra insisted that Aburi must stand. Aburi is the place where the meeting was held in Ghana. Biafra was formed by the then leader of the faction. This war claimed so many lives, especially from the side of the Biafran population. It was an unjust war from the Nigerian side that resulted from greed and wickedness. After almost three years, with many lives and properties destroyed, the war ended on the agreement of 'no victor, no vanquish' on 15 January 1970. Could this war not have been avoided? Yes, it could have been. There is still an element of hidden acrimony between the Igbo, Yoruba, and Hausa tribes. What is good about wars? Nothing, really. If we love each other and value each other, we will not fight but we will dialogue and negotiate until a mutual agreement is reached, regardless of how long it would take.

Scotland and England

I will not write on this because I voted no and campaigned for no during the referendum. Why should the war of hatred, fought for so many years before our grandparents were born, be taught in schools for our children to live in perpetual hatred? I will never support it. It is troubling for me when Christians are also involved in this hatred. Scots against the English and the English against the Scots. First John 4: 20–21 says, 'You cannot love God whom you do not see if you don't love the person whom you see.'

I want my children to be taught about the Battle of Bannockburn, 24 June 1314, as Scottish history and not to hate or see England as the enemy of Scotland.

CHAPTER 10

Mr Ebola, a Curable Disease

I gave this disease the title of 'Mister Ebola', and it does not have a real meaning in African culture. So where did the name come from? I wish I could answer the question. The name Ebola is a name fabricated by the medical experts. Probably after a few years, the Ebola saga will pass, and another disease will appear. And of course, another name will be given. This disease started from West Africa, and the whole world is practically in frenzy about it so that many countries, including the United Kingdom, have quickly put some rules in place to check the passengers coming from West African countries. The media has successfully instilled serious fear in the public. In some West African countries, people are even afraid of hugging or shaking someone's hands. Is this Ebola that powerful that it could just kill anyone who touches a carrier? Not really. So why is the media spreading this bad news as if everyone is going to get it? If you look at a story of an Ebola carrier, newspapers and magazines are sold more during tragedies, and our media stays open around the clock. That's why children's educational programmes don't attract high audience. What a pity. As of today, 7 November 2014, we heard that Mr Ebola has killed about five thousand people. Companies and some charities are capitalizing on Mr Ebola to raise money for their organizations and not for Ebola sufferers. It is on record that generally people donate when there is a disaster or an outbreak of a disease like Ebola. Majority of the money raised will not leave UK for Africa, and that has been proven when charities used the money that was raised for 'third-world countries' for their staff salaries and overheads.

Hunger in West Africa is killing more people than Ebola has killed so far. What is the world doing? Hunger is a preventable sickness. A man who is hungry does not need paracetamol; he needs food.

A child who is dying of malnutrition needs a healthy balanced diet. Why are we projecting Ebola out of proposition when cancer is killing more people than Ebola would ever kill? Our statistics in United Kingdom show that someone dies of cancer every day, but no one has died of Ebola yet. According to 2014 Macmillan Cancer Support, by 2016, 32,270 people will be dealing with the news of cancer each year. It means about ninety Scots will be diagnosed with the disease in a single day. We should not ignore Ebola, but we should not really ignore the hungry in the border of Turkey and Syria where thousands are begging daily for food. In the UK, people and shops throw away food every day while people are dying, and they can be saved by our leftovers.

How will UK government cope if Mr Ebola enters the country? Can you imagine one Ebola sufferer in a packed London Underground, one at a packed football stadium, or one on a school bus? In my experience, this October 2014 puts doubt in my mind about the British government's readiness to tackle Ebola in the UK.

Nigerian Government

I went to Nigeria/West Africa on 20 October 2014 after the World Health Organization (WHO) had declared Nigeria Ebola-free. When we arrived at Lagos International Airport, every passenger, including the pilots and cabin staff, was tested. We were given forms to fill inside the plane that asked some questions such as 'Any health issues? Feeling any symptoms? Countries visited before arriving?' etc. On arrival, the form was collected and our temperatures were taken before going to immigration. I was very impressed with the way the Nigerian government was tackling the problem while in cities, towns, and some villages, people were being educated about sanitation. In hotels, before you approach the reception area, a liquid is poured into your hands before you enter. I felt very safe in the largest country in Africa. On my way coming back to the UK before we went to check in at the counter, we were given another form to fill by the health staff with questions such as 'Where did you visit? Did you attend any funeral? What kind of gathering did you attend?' Before we got to immigration, the forms were collected by the health authority, and our temperatures were taken again. Then our boarding cards were stamped to show that we had been tested and cleared to board the plane. It was meticulously done, and I praise the government of President Goodluck Jonathan. He cannot be faulted on this issue. He executed and handled Mr Ebola with force and first-class strategy. Surprisingly I flew into Amsterdam from Lagos, mingled with many people at the airport for hours, and boarded the plane to Edinburgh International Airport, and there was no checking of any kind. I just waited for my bags, collected them, and off I went. I came back and went to our Friday church service.

Ebola is both curable and healable. Since God can heal the sick and can raise the dead, he can also heal Ebola. All of us must be health cautious; hygiene should be on the mind of everyone. There are some things we eat and drink that can pose serious risk to our health. Prevention is better than cure. You have only one life. Bacteria can travel in seconds without notice. Our children should be taught simple hygiene, such as washing of hands before and after food and after playing, brushing of teeth regularly, and taking a shower. These simple tips can help.

A lot has been said and written about Ebola. Some have been accurate and fair while a lot has been overexaggerated. This will not be the first time that a disease has been overdramatized. For example, many years ago, salmonella was given so much publicity, and the public was told not to eat eggs in the United Kingdom. Another was mad cow disease. This also was overexaggerated, and again, the public was asked to avoid eating beef. Ebola has dominated the world news just like AIDS did for many years, and no one talks much about it now.

I submit that these diseases—salmonella, mad cow disease, AIDS, and Ebola—are serious and contagious and transmittable, but they can never be compared to diabetes and cancer. Untold wealth is being spent by different countries and by scientists to find a cure for cancer but to no avail. I believe that the medical experts are doing their best, working hard to find a cure, and I sincerely hope they find a cure soon. I have read many articles and have spoken to cancer patients and their families who did not only dread the disease but also the pain of chemotherapy and radiotherapy. They claim that these treatments are more painful than the disease itself. As a minister who visits hospitals to comfort and pray for the sick, I sincerely believe that cancer is the worst disease from hell. It is a disease that can affect almost every part of human anatomy. We hear of cancer of the brain, uterus, ovary, skin, throat, bowel, etc.

Ebola was discovered in four West African countries, and in a few months, the World Health Organization (WHO) cleared one of the countries—Nigeria—Ebola-free. But WHO cannot clear any country in the world of cancer. The medical experts tell patients who were cured of cancer not to raise their hopes because it could reoccur, and in some cases, it does. If a person or a country can be declared free of Ebola, just like the British nurse who contracted the disease while helping Ebola victims in West Africa and was cured in January 2015, that means that Ebola is curable. Ebola is contracted by physical contact, but cancer is not. Nurses and doctors who work in cancer wards do not contract the disease simply by working in those wards.

The latest publication in February 2015 states the following:

> One in two people will develop cancer as some point in their lives and the UK faces 'crisis' if the NHS does not plan ahead, according to the latest forecast.

> There will 'never be one single magic bullet' to cure all cancers and age is the biggest risk factor for most forms of the disease.

> The new figure, which replaces the previous one in three, is the most accurate forecast to date from Cancer in Research UK and is published in the *British Journal of Cancer*.

> The charity said it highlights the urgent need to bolster public health and NHS cancer services so they can cope with a growing and ageing population and the looming demands for better diagnostics, treatments and earlier diagnosis.

> Prevention must also play a role in the effort required to reduce the impact of the disease in coming decades, the charity said.

> The UK's cancer survival rate has doubled over the last 40 years and around half of patients now survive the disease for more than 10 years.

> This new research estimating lifetime risk replaces the previous figure, calculated using a different method, which predicted that more than one in three people would develop cancer at some point in their lives.

The charity said age is the biggest risk factor for most cancers, and the increase in lifetime risk is primarily because more people are surviving into old age, when cancer is more common.

The results show that people who were born in 1930 had a lifetime risk of just over one in three, but the risk has risen to one in two for those born in 1960.

The lifetime cancer risk for women (47.55%) is lower than that of men (53.5%), while the combined lifetime risk is 50.5%.

While the biggest risk factor is age, other lifestyle factors include smoking, obesity, diet, tanning and sunburn, overdiagnosis, lack of exercise and child-bearing patterns.
Just over a quarter of all deaths are caused by cancer, so while one in two people will develop cancer at some point, it is still believed that around one in four people will die from cancer.
Harpal Kumar, Cancer Research UK's chief executive, said, 'If the NHS doesn't act and invest now, we will face a crisis in the future—with outcomes from cancer going backwards.'

I pray that God will enable our medical experts to find a cure for the disease from hell called cancer.

CHAPTER 11

The Scottish Referendum, 18 September 2014

Before the nation casted her vote, the Scottish National Party, led by the first secretary Alex Salmond MP, told the nation during campaigning that majority wanted independence. The leaders of the three main political parties rushed into Scotland and were going from city to city, town to town, village to village, and in some areas, door to door. The eyes of the world were on the United Kingdom. Some people within the United Kingdom were scared of what might be—Scotland leaving the United Kingdom. But I and members of our church knew that the Scottish National Party was not representing us in saying that the majority of Scots wanted independence. The nation was on the edge. Mr Salmond and his party fought and managed to reduce the age of voting from eighteen years to sixteen years in order to get more vote for his mission for independence. But it still did not materialize. The number of votes was the highest in the history of Scotland. Before the votes were cast on 18 September 2014, I wrote an article published in our local newspapers, the *Courier* and *Fife Fire Press*, titled 'God Is in the Union'. I knew that God did not want Scotland to separate from the United Kingdom. I was criticized by many, and a few newspapers rejected the article, but at the end, the yes campaign lost, and the no campaign won. The SNP based their support for independence on the oil from Scotland. How could such an argument hold when no human could determine how long the oil would last and how stable the oil price could be?

Respect for Mr Salmond

What a politician! I will call him a man of timbre and calibre, an intelligent politician who loves Scotland dearly with his blood. But I was glad when he resigned as the leader of the SNP and as our first secretary because his well-spent hard-fought ambition of independence failed. Had he won the referendum, he would not have resigned his post. I also believe that Mr Salmond is needed in London as an MP. I will urge the people to vote for him, and I know that he will win the seat. The promises made by London to Scotland must be fulfilled, and no one better than Mr Salmond to make London keep to the promises of the agreement signed by the three political leaders, Mr David Cameron (Conservative Party), Mr Nick Clegg (Liberal Democrat), and Ed Miliband (Labour Party).

The Oil Revenue Low Price (January 2015)

God is in the Union

Four months after vote for independence the oil price has tumbled from more than $100 per barrel to less than $50 since the summer 2014, of which the governor of Bank of England, Mr. Mark Carney said was the lowest in six years. Scotland would have been in a near catastrophe if the nation had voted 'YES' to independence.

Financial experts have said that the plunge in oil prices could cause up to 35,000 job losses. We in Zion Praise Centre International are thanking God for not allowing the 'YES' campaign to wind.

(*Courier* and *Fife Free Press*, 18 September 2014)

GOD IS IN THE UNION

DIVIDED WE WILL FALL, AND UNITED WE WILL STAND

Unity brings strength in a marriage, at home, in the workplace, in business, and in the church. God Almighty, in his infinite grace, united Scotland with England when James VI became James I and united the kingdoms. This was not just the work of a political movement. It should be also called an act of God. Ever since the union, we have lived together and survived together.

WHY TRY TO FIX SOMETHING THAT IS NOT BROKEN?

There are other issues that the SNP should concentrate on that are affecting poor people's lives.

The referendum can be seen as a slave seeking to separate from the slave master, but this is not the case here. Independence is good when it is motivated by love and honesty, and for the well-being of the nation. But this is not the case here. The majority do not want it, but it is forced on the nation. This is purely an idea, a dream, an ambition of our first secretary. If it works out, he will take the credit, but if it fails, he will pass it off as a political mistake. There is no good parent who will gamble on the future of their children into the unknown. Does Scotland need independence? No! Why not? Because we are safer, stronger, and richer within the union. For example, no country will initiate war against Scotland because that country will fear the might and power of the United Kingdom.

We are kingdoms united by God.

All the church ministers in Scotland should pray and seek the counsel of God in this issue and advise the congregation accordingly how to and how not to vote. I have prayed and advised our people what I believe God is saying. I am proud to announce that I will be voting *no*. Some business CEOs and church ministers are afraid to let their people know which way they are voting.

In the early Bible days, the church did not go seeking advice on matters of the day from politicians. Politicians and rulers went to the church to hear 'Thus says the Lord.' For instance, King Solomon, the man known for wisdom.

We need rulers; we need politicians—we are instructed to pray for them so that they can be effective in what they do (1 Timothy 2:1–4). If we all vote yes on the 18th and later realize that we have made a terrible mistake, what do we do then? We put the future of millions of born and unborn in danger. But if we all vote *no* on the 18th, we will not make any mistake, because we are still in the United Kingdom.

In the *Daily Record* of June 2, the former prime minister listed the names of great Scots who changed the world. These people were given great gifts and talents by God. Those well-known like John Knox or the less well-known like Mary Slessor, who, by the wisdom of God, stopped the killing of twins in Africa. Men like Andrew Carnegie, Adam Smith, and Alexander Fleming did not change the world with oil revenue.

Why does the SNP want to divide the union? It must be known that oil revenue will not last. How can our first secretary place our future on uncertainties?

MESSAGE FOR THE PRIME MINISTER

Mr David Cameron should consult with the other party leaders and sign a joint agreement to transfer significant powers to Scotland following the next elections to increase powers in tax, education, health, and the economics of employment. There are many ways to ensure that the vote will be *no*. I do not want to be in a position where I need my passport to visit my sister in Birmingham.

As a minister of the gospel, I am very proud to know the history of the King James Bible announced first in Burntisland. Scotland became known as the Land of the Book. God did not place the oil in our waters in order to separate us. We are stronger together, safer together, richer together.

CHAPTER 12

Can Britain Be Great Again?

Is there still hope for us in Britain? Yes, I believe there is if we will rethink and return to God, whom we once knew and served. The hearts of so many people in United Kingdom, even children, are hardened. The things that were once considered a shocking abomination are generally seen as normal and are no longer shocking to people such as husbands and wives planning to kill each other, someone being beheaded, parents stabbing their children repeatedly with a knife, someone planting a bomb in a crowded bus or hotel, people committing suicide, or people in positions of authorities looting public funds in an alarming proportion, just to mention a few. The kinds of hearts that think and commit these kinds of atrocities are never those who are homeless or the 'nobodies' in the society. We have read and seen where the lawmakers have been sent to prison for breaking the same laws. Every offence or sin that a person commits starts from the heart. It must be conceived in the heart first before being put to action. For example, no one wakes up in the morning and becomes a terrorist. They conceive it, think about it, and decide whether that lifestyle is for them or not. It doesn't matter whether they were brainwashed or not, and the same goes for an armed robber. As a minister of the Gospel of Jesus Christ who travels extensively, I have noticed that Britain is not an exception. It is worse in some other countries where the rule of law is ignored and corruption is an everyday affair. Britain colonized many nations and brought civilization and religion to many nations, sent missionaries to many countries. So she must be the leader as charity begins at home. You cannot give someone what you don't have. The almighty God stopped a small crisis from happening in Britain by Scots voting no to the 18 September 2014 Scottish Referendum. If the majority had voted yes, the foundation of Britain would have been dealt big cracks, and who knows what would have followed next? No one political party can take credit for the victory against the referendum.

Before I came from Nigeria, Africa, to live in the United Kingdom, I had heard and read about great godly men and women from Britain such as John Wesley, the Jeffrey Brothers, John Knox, Smith Wigglesworth, Mary Slessor, David Livingstone, and Florence Nightingale. These people took the love, peace, and the power of God to the world. Why has Britain turned her back from God? In my opinion, *wickedness* and *materialism* are the primary reasons. The love and reverence of God has been given to idolatry, hence the consequences that we are facing today. But God is merciful and just. He can pardon and restore the glory days if we return from our rebellious ways. Once known as the nation of the Bible, it is now known as the nation of *bribery*. God said in the Bible, 'If my people who are called by my name shall humble themselves and pray and seek my face and turn from their wicked ways, then I will hear from heaven and will forgive their sin and will heal their land' (2 Chronicles 7:14). What else do we need to hear? Whether we believe it or not, God Almighty has the final say to avoid the time bomb from exploding in the United Kingdom. We must adhere to the above warning from God. If you can change the hearts of people, you can change their actions either positively or negatively.

> The Lord brings the counsel of the nations to nothing; He makes the plans of the peoples of no effect. The counsel of the Lord stands forever, the plans of His heart to all generations. Blessed is the nation whose God is the Lord, the people He has chosen as His own inheritance. (Psalm 33:10–12)

I believe that Britain can be great again only if the leaders of the nation will adhere to, believe, and implement the advice of God in the Bible. I know that the words *freedom of speech* and *human rights* will come up again. Some have said openly that they don't believe in God, or they question if there is a God, while others claim that they don't need God in their lives. Can a baby say that he or she does not need their mother? Science will continue to fail in regard to the deity and existence of God.

The Almighty God was in existence before science, and that is why he is the Creator. If Britain worships science, the consequences cannot be measured.

The safety and the success of a nation or an organization is not only measured by the economy but by the vision of the leadership of that nation or organization. The nation that used to lead the world is now being led by those she once led. Jesus Christ prophesied about all the things that are happening in the world today over two thousand years ago.

> And you will hear of wars and rumors of wars. See that you are not troubled; for all these things must come to pass, but the end is not yet. For nation will rise against nation, and kingdom against kingdom. And there will be famines, pestilences, and earthquakes in various places. All these are the beginning of sorrows. (Matthew 24:6–8)

How long can we continue to be stubborn? Can we not read the writing on the wall? It's even difficult for one political party to win an election in Britain in this twenty-first century. How much longer will the light continue to shine in Britain before it is dimmed? Should Britain continue to take the mercy of God for granted?

> It is of the Lord's mercies that we are not consumed, because his compassions fail not. (Lamentations 3:22, KJV)

To whom much is given, much is required.

THE VISION AND MISSION.

The Vision which God gave to Pastor Joe Nwokoye, is directly from the Bible in Isaiah 58 verses 6-11 and Isaiah 61 verses 1-3. He has taken this on board since he was ordained as a minister of the gospel in Nigeria. Pastor Joe is of the opinion that poverty has no coloure, race and boundaries. As directed, he has and still training people from primary School, High School, College and university, many whose parents have died or are not able to train their children. As the president and founder of Zion Bible Institute, a theological institution with affiliations in the United States of America, is giving full scholarships to Diploma and Degree students. He has programs to feed and house the needy. The photographs will explain just some of the many humanitarian activities which goes on in his ministry. Pastor Joe strongly believe that the governments alone should not be left with helping humanity. It is not a work of a man, but God working through a man-says pastor Joe.

The Egeh Children

The Osuke Children

The Okoye Children

The Okafor Children

Michael

Angel and her Daughter

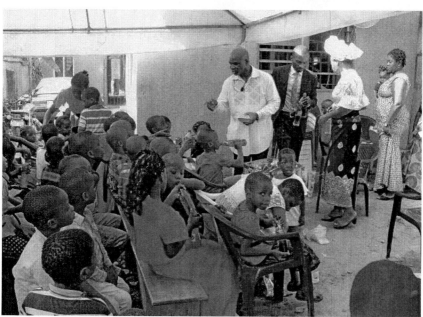

Pastor Joe & team feeding the children

Bible School Students/ Lecturers

Bible schools students graduating

Some of the beneficiaries

Joel and Jethro Nwokoye

Jessica and Joseph Nwokoye

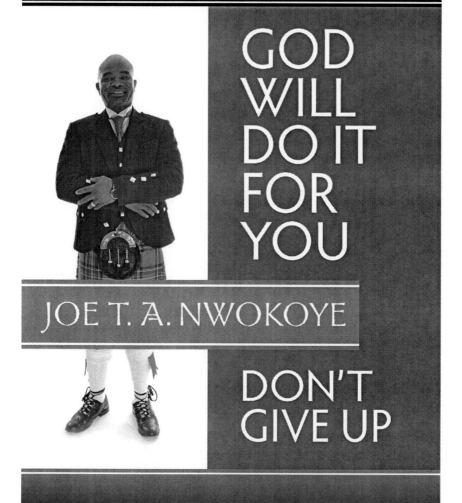

God Will Do It For You

Can be ordered from Amazon.com, Burns and Noble, and Lifeway.com

ZION PRAISE CENTRE INTERNATIONAL INC.
44 Mitchell Street
Kirkcaldy KY1 1BD
Fife County
SCOTLAND, UNITED KINGDOM
Tel: +44 159 226 2209
Email: *zif@btinternet.com*
Web: *www.zionpraisecenter.org*

Lightning Source UK Ltd.
Milton Keynes UK
UKOW04f0018300415

250590UK00001B/41/P